FASHION ORIGAMI

ORIGAMI OUTFITS

A Foldable Fashion Guide

by SOK SONG

CAPSTONE PRESS
a capstone imprint

GUIDE TO FOLDING

Making crisp, accurate creases is the key to a clean and polished origami model. Use these lines and symbols to help you and guide your creases. Don't worry if you've made a mistake or something seems confusing—just back up a couple of steps and try again.

LINES AND DASHES

 VALLEY FOLD

 MOUNTAIN FOLD

 CREASE LINE

 HIDDEN LINE

ACTION SYMBOLS

 FOLD

 PLEAT

MAGNIFIED VIEW

 FOLD AND UNFOLD

 REPEAT

ROTATE

 UNFOLD

 TURN OVER

DISTANCE

FOLD BEHIND
(MOUNTAIN FOLD)

 SQUASH

° ° FOCAL POINTS

DIFFICULTY LEVEL

♟♟♟ EASY   ♟♟♟ MEDIUM   ♟♟♟ CHALLENGING

COMMON FOLDS

VALLEY FOLD

Fold the paper to the front so the crease is pointing away from you, like a valley.

MOUNTAIN FOLD

Fold the paper to the back so the crease is pointing up at you, like a mountain.

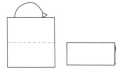

SQUASH FOLD

Open the pocket and squash down flat. Most often, this will be done on the existing pre-creases.

INSIDE REVERSE FOLD

Fold the flap or corner to the inside, reversing one of the creases.

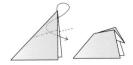

OUTSIDE REVERSE FOLD

Fold the flap or corner to the outside, reversing one of the creases.

PLEAT FOLD

Fold the paper to create a pleat.

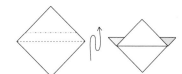

TABLE OF CONTENTS

SHIFT DRESS

Shift dresses are easy to wear and a simple, classic wardrobe must-have for any fashionista. Although this paper version has a slightly nipped-in waist to give it shape, most shift dresses have no defined waist. That's why it's important to find one that fits correctly. Look for a dress that's neither boxy nor tight. A fun pattern or bright color can also make your dress stand out!

STYLE TIPS

- A simple shift dress can be dressed up or down—throw on a blazer or sweater for a more professional look, or add a casual jacket and flats for the perfect weekend outfit.

- Add some statement jewelry—like a bangle or necklace—to dress up your shift dress.

4

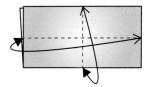

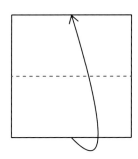

Fold the paper in half horizontally.
(Note: The side facing down will
become the outside of your shift dress.)

Fold in half again in both
directions and then unfold.

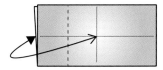

Fold the left side into the center
crease and then unfold.

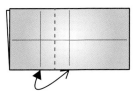

Fold from crease to crease
(between the quarter and half
creases) and then unfold.

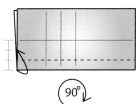

Fold the bottom edge up one-third
of the way between the bottom of
the paper and the center crease.
(Note: You can experiment with
what happens to the center of your
shift dress depending on the width
of this fold.) Rotate the paper 90°.

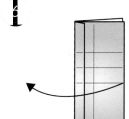

Unfold the paper back
to the original square.

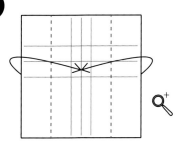

Fold the side edges into the
center on the existing
pre-creases. (Note: the next
step is a magnified view.)

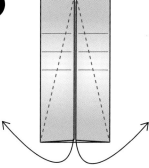

Fold the bottom corners out at
an angle starting from the top
center point. (See the next step
for reference.)

9

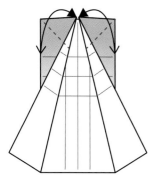

Using just the top layer of paper, fold the corners down at a 45° angle and then unfold. (Note: The corners will line up with the side folded edges.)

10

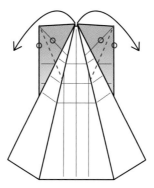

Fold the corner out to make the sleeves of your dress by lining up the crease from the previous step with the side folded edges. (See the next step for reference.)

11

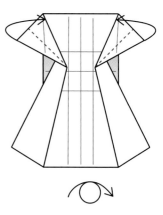

Angle bisect the triangle from the bottom point to make the sleeves smaller. Turn the paper over.

12

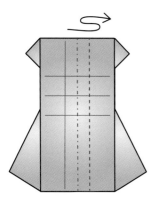

Pleat fold the center using the existing crease. (See the next step for reference.)

13

Make a new valley crease between the top two pre-creases and then unfold.

14

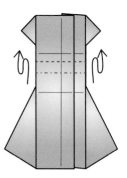

Pleat fold the center using the crease made in the previous step and the lower pre-crease. (Note: The mountain crease is on the bottom, and the valley crease is on top. See the next step for reference.)

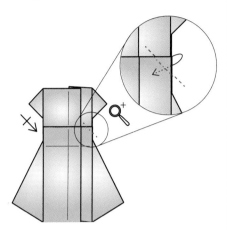

Fold and unfold, then inside reverse the small corner to taper the dress and bodice. Repeat on the opposite side.

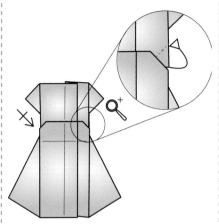

Mountain fold the small corner on the back layer. Repeat on the opposite side.

Fold and unfold, then inside reverse the top of the bodice in an asymmetrical diagonal. (Note: This is to shape the top of the garment. See the next step for reference.)

Mountain fold the upper corner of the back layer to finish shaping the V-neck.

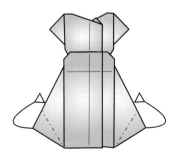

Mountain fold the bottom corners to shape the skirt.

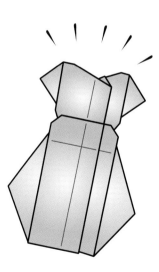

Enjoy your finished shift dress!

SUNDRESS

Sundresses are the perfect summer attire—they're easy to wear, lightweight, and comfortable. Plus they come in a variety of fun, playful patterns. This paper version features a feminine floral print, but you can play around with an array of other patterns as well. For the most flattering fit, look for a sundress that hits at or just above the knee. A fitted waist, like the one on this model, also helps create an elegant silhouette.

STYLE TIPS

⊕ Pair your sundress with a pair of heels to make it party-ready, or opt for a pair of flip-flops or flat sandals for a more casual look.

⊕ Don't forget your shades! Nothing completes a summer look like a cute pair of sunglasses.

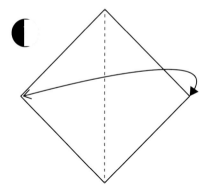

1

Fold the paper in half diagonally and then unfold. (Note: The side that is facing down will become the pattern of your sundress.)

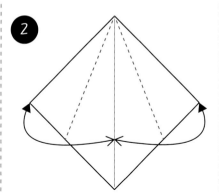

2

Fold the sides into the center crease and then unfold.

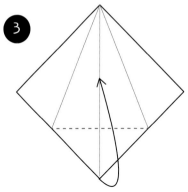

3

Fold the bottom triangle up using the bottom edge of the pre-creases made in the previous step as a landmark.

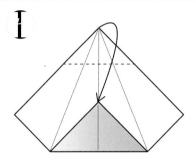

4

Fold the top corner down to meet the tip of the bottom corner.

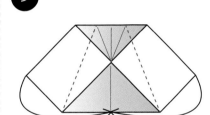

5

Fold the sides back in on the pre-creases made in step #2.

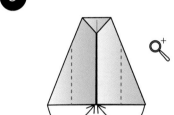

6

Fold the side corners into the center on the bottom. Be careful that the layers of paper don't shift. (Note: The next step is a magnified view.)

7

Turn the paper over.

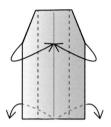

8

Fold the side edges into the center, allowing the corner flaps to flip out to the front as you make this crease. (See the next step for reference.)

9

Mountain fold the top section to the back, using the circled points for reference. The crease will be slightly below where the top corners of the triangle meet.

10

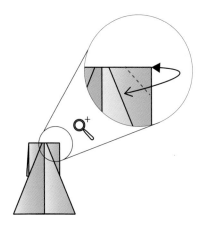

Fold and then unfold a small triangle on the top right corner. (See magnified view for reference.)

11

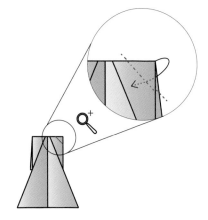

Inside reverse the corner.

12

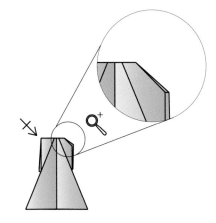

Repeat on the opposite side.

13

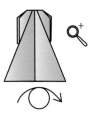

Turn the paper over. (Note: The next step is a magnified view.)

14

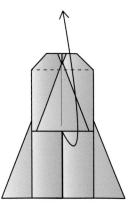

Fold up the flap at the base of the inside-reversed triangles.

15

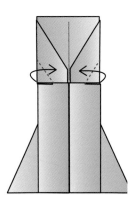

Fold in small triangles at each bottom corner. This will create a separation between the bodice and the skirt. (Note: You can taper it at more of an angle if you would like.)

16

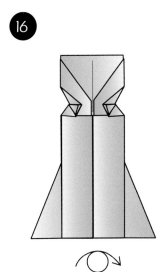

Turn the paper back over to the front.

17

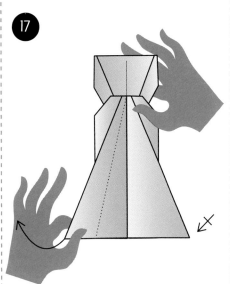

Hold the dress in the middle section near the right side as you pull the bottom left corner to spread the dress open wider. Repeat on the opposite side.

18

Optional: Mountain fold the top section in a V-line, similar to an inside reverse, to give the bodice more shape.

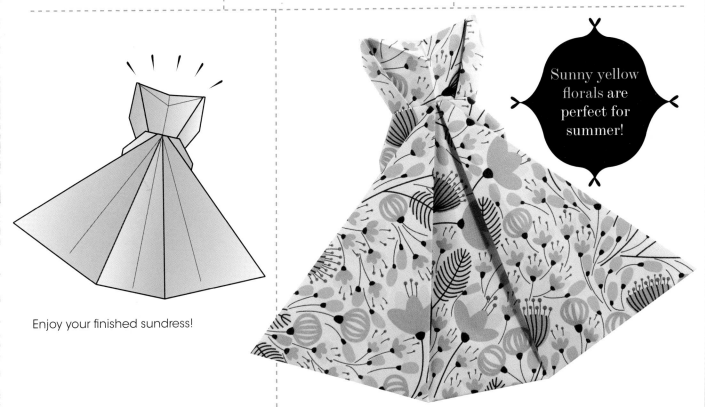

Enjoy your finished sundress!

Sunny yellow florals are perfect for summer!

PROM DRESS

The dress you wear to prom has to be just right—the right color, the right shape, the right fabric, and the right style! This paper **prom dress** has an elegant sweetheart neckline and just the right amount of flair in the skirt! Try folding it with contrasting colors on each side to make it pop and play up the color change.

STYLE TIPS

- Pair your prom dress with a fun pair of high heels in a contrasting hue for a bright pop of color.

- Make sure to grab a fun bag—like a stylish purse or clutch—to hold all your belongings.

How To Fold

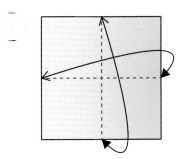

Fold the paper in half in both directions and unfold. (Note: The side facing up will become the outside of your prom dress; the side facing down will become the contrasting neckline.)

Fold the top edge down to the center crease.

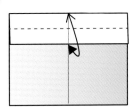

Fold the edge back up to the top and then unfold.

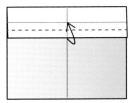

Fold the bottom edge up to the new crease made in the previous step.

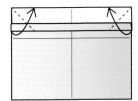

Fold the outside corners in, lining up the outside edge with the top of the paper.

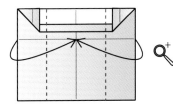

Fold the side edges into the center crease. (Note: The next step is a magnified view.)

Turn the paper over.

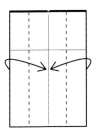

Fold the sides into the center crease.

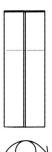

Turn the paper over.

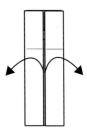

Open the front flaps back out to the sides.

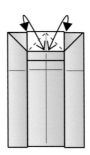

Using only the color-change section at the top, fold the top corners down and then unfold.

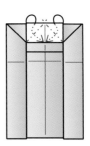

Inside reverse the corners using the pre-creases made in the previous step.

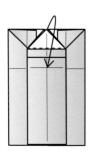

Fold the top triangle flap down.

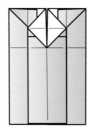

Turn the paper over.

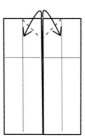

Fold the center corners down, using the pre-crease as a reference. (Note: There will be a small colored triangle in the back layer that also needs to be folded down. See the next step for reference.)

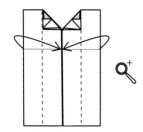

Reverse the existing pre-creases and fold the sides into the center. (Note: The next step is a magnified view.)

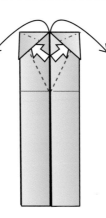

Open and squash the pockets at the top, using the pre-existing horizontal crease as a reference for the diagonal. This will be an asymmetrical squash fold. (See the next step for reference.)

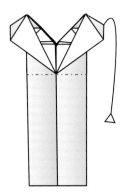

18 Mountain fold the top section to the back on the existing pre-crease.

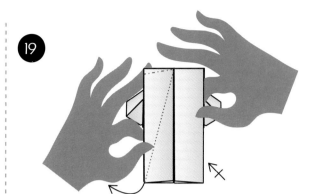

19 Pinch the upper right corner as you slide the front layer out from the bottom left corner, making a new diagonal crease. Repeat on the opposite side.

20 Fold the top layer flaps out at an angle, widening the skirt.

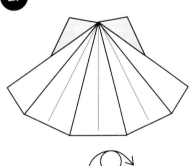

21 Turn the paper over.

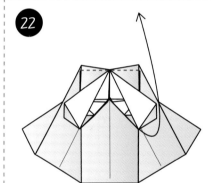

22 Fold the front section back up to the top on the existing pre-crease.

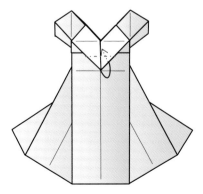

23 Optional: You can either leave the top section as a heart shape or tuck the bottom corner under the pocket below.

Enjoy your finished prom dress!

LITTLE BLACK DRESS

The **LBD**—also known as the **little black dress**—is an absolute must for any fashionista's closet. The perfect LBD is both timeless and versatile, but finding a dress that stands out from the crowd is equally important. The asymmetrical details on both the skirt and bodice of this paper LBD help set it apart from your basic black dress, and the tapered waist makes for an extra flattering fit.

STYLE TIPS

- Don't forget the accessories—bold jewelry and a chic clutch to carry all your evening essentials are a must!

- Pair your LBD with a stylish pair of high heels for a full-on fancy ensemble.

Pg. 24

1

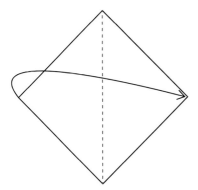

Fold the paper in half diagonally. (Note: The side facing down will become the outside of the dress.)

2

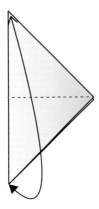

Fold the paper in half horizontally and then unfold.

3

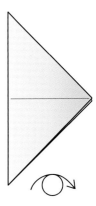

Turn the paper over.

4

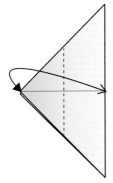

Fold the left corner to the opposite edge and then unfold.

5

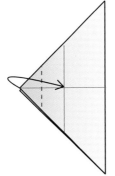

Fold the left corner (through both layers of paper) into the crease created in the previous step.

6

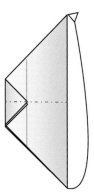

Mountain fold the paper in half on the existing pre-crease by folding the bottom corner to the back.

7

Fold the paper in half, bringing the left edge across to the opposite side. (Note: The next step is a magnified view.)

8

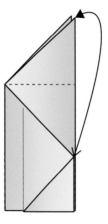

Fold the top corner down, through all layers, and then unfold. (Note: Use the upper point of the left triangle as a reference.)

9

Turn the paper over.

10

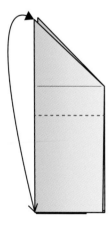

Valley fold the top corner down to the bottom and then unfold.

11

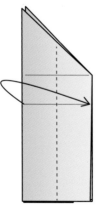

Valley fold the tall left side (the top double layers of paper) in half. (Note: This will leave the shorter bottom section in the back.)

12

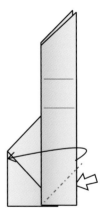

Open and squash fold by bringing only the top layer of the right side back to the left side. A pocket will open on the bottom to squash into an upside-down triangle. (See the next step for reference.)

13

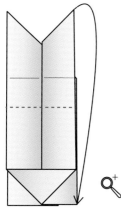

Valley fold the model in half horizontally using the preexisting crease. (Note: The next step is a magnified view.)

14

Pre-crease and inside reverse the upper left and right corners.

15

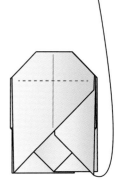

Fold the top layer back up on the existing crease to create the bodice of the dress. (See the next step for reference.)

16

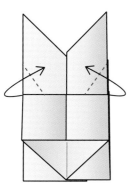

Valley fold the lower left and right corners of the bodice to shape the waistline of the dress.

17

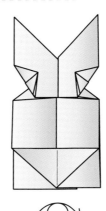

Turn the paper over.

18

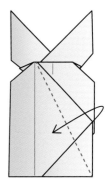

Valley fold the loose flap on the top front layer of the skirt.

19

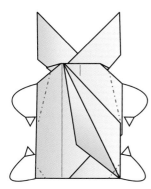

Mountain fold the upper and lower corners of the skirt to the back to shape the bottom of the dress.

Enjoy your finished LBD!

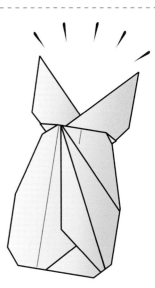

BALL GOWN

A **ball gown** can be a lot of things—classic, simple, elegant, beautiful, and timeless—but no matter what, it's always the perfect piece for a special formal occasion. With a bold skirt and art deco-inspired bodice, this paper version captures all those qualities and more. Feel free to jazz it up with glitter, jewels, and bling to make it even more special!

STYLE TIPS

- Dress your ball gown up with a pretty pair of high heels.

- Don't forget to grab a clutch to hold all your evening essentials!

1

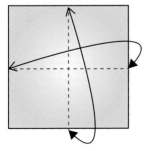

Fold the paper in half in both directions and then unfold. (Note: The side facing up will become the bottom of the ball gown; the opposite side will become the bodice.)

2

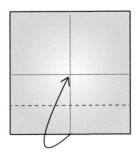

Fold the bottom edge up to the center crease made in the previous step.

3

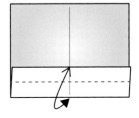

Fold the bottom edge, now two layers thick, up again to the meet the center crease. Then unfold the paper back to the original square.

4

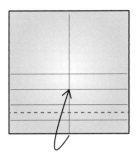

Fold the bottom edge up, using the third crease from the bottom as a landmark. (See the next step for reference.)

5

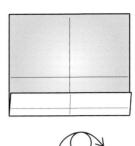

Turn the paper over.

6

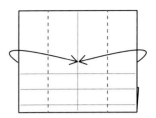

Fold both side edges into the center. (Note: The next step is a magnified view.)

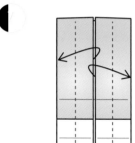

Fold the edges back out to the sides.

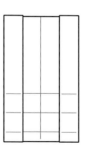

Turn the paper over.

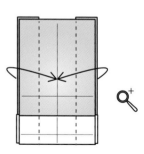

Fold both sides into the center. There will now be many pleated layers. (Note: The next step is a magnified view.)

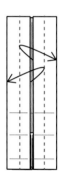

Fold only the top layers out to the sides. (See the next step for reference.)

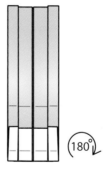

Rotate the paper 180° so the color-changed section is at the top. This top section is the bodice of the dress.

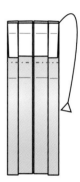

Mountain fold the top section behind on the existing pre-crease in preparation for folding the bottom section of the dress.

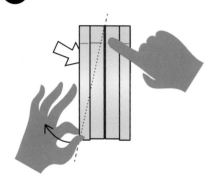

Pinch the bottom left corner and spread open to shape the dress. Make a new crease, pulling as far as you can without tearing the paper. It will help to hold down the top right side of the paper. (Note: Keep the model flat on the table and only lift the left side as you spread-squash.)

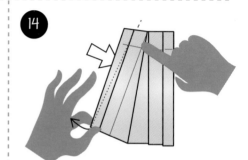

Spread-squash the small section on the edge, similar to the last step. (Note: It will help to hold down the right section.)

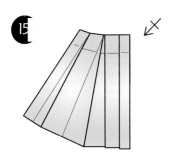

15 Repeat the spread-squashes from steps #13–14 on the opposite side.

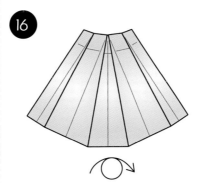

16 Turn the paper over.

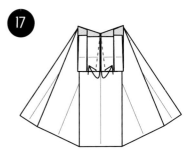

17 Fold the inner folded edges of the bodice in at a diagonal.

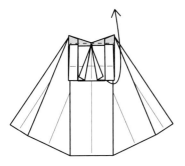

18 Fold the top section back up while keeping the spread-squashed parts of the dress flat.

19 Fold the top corners to shape the bodice of the dress. (Note: There are three folded corner layers. If it's too thick to fold them all at once, you can fold them in one at a time.)

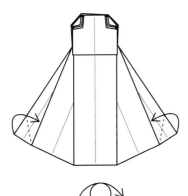

20 Fold the bottom corners to shape the skirt and turn the paper over.

Enjoy your finished ball gown! (Note: You can shape the ball gown as you'd like, making the skirt and bodice of the dress fuller or more tapered, depending on your personal taste.)

HIGH HEELS

Formal and elegant, the right **high heels** can take your outfit to new heights—literally! This simple paper version has a color-change geometric bow shape in the front and can be folded with many different patterns and colors. After all, you can never have too many pairs of fabulous shoes!

STYLE TIPS

- Pair your heels with jeans or skinny pants and a dressy blouse for a fun night out. Just make sure to choose heels that are comfortable!

- High heels are the perfect choice to wear with a ball gown, prom dress, or little black dress for a formal occasion.

How To Fold

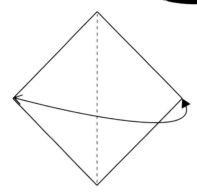

Fold the paper in half diagonally and then unfold. (Note: The side facing down will become the outside of the heels; the side facing up will become the contrasting bow.)

2

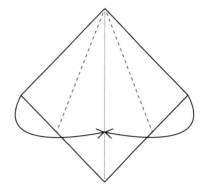

Fold the side edges into the center crease.

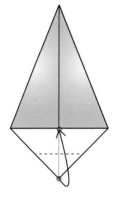

Fold the tip of the bottom triangle up to the contrasting edge.

4

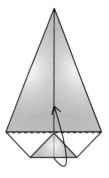

Fold the bottom section up at the contrasting edge.

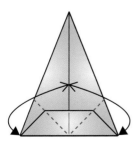

Fold the bottom corners up and into the center crease and then unfold.

6

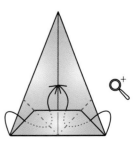

Inside reverse the corners. (Note: The next step is a magnified view.)

7

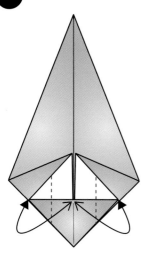

Using just the top layer of paper, fold the side corners into the center and then unfold.

8

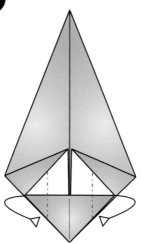

Mountain fold the corners to the back on the crease made in the previous step. (Note: This is not an inside reverse. Just fold and tuck to the back.)

9

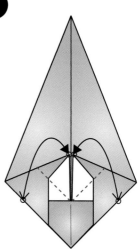

Fold the corners down and then unfold. (Note: Use the circled points for reference.)

10

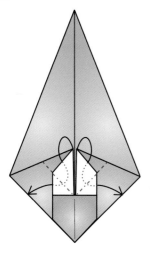

Inside reverse the points on the existing pre-creases.

11

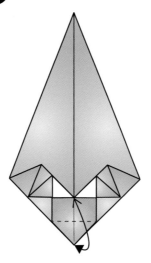

Fold the bottom corner up and then unfold.

12

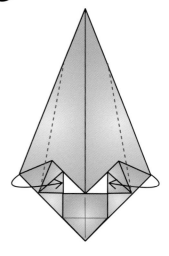

Fold the sides in. The side corners will align with the outside edges of the contrasting triangles. (See the next step for reference.)

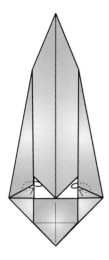

Tuck the bottom corners
underneath the bi-colored
triangular flaps.

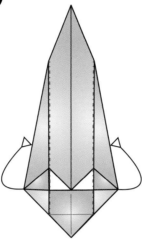

Mountain fold the sides
to the back.

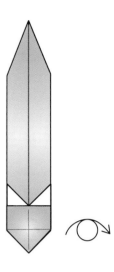

Turn the paper over.

Fold the top corner
down to the indicated
point and then unfold.

Fold the top corner down,
halfway between the crease
made in the previous step and
the top of the paper. (Use the
circled points for reference.)

Narrow the sides of
the top section.

19

Fold the top down on
the existing pre-crease.

20

Mountain fold all the layers in
half vertically on the existing
pre-crease in the center.

21

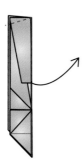

Pull the heel of the shoe out at
an angle. You can change the
angle depending on how high
you want the heel to be. (See
the next step for reference.)

22

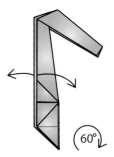

Gently pull the sides open to
shape the front of the shoe
and rotate the model 60°.

23

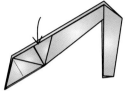

Open the inside of the shoe in the front and pull the side edges down to shape the shoe. (See the next step for reference.)

24

Using the existing pre-crease, fold the small triangle at the tip back slightly to help shape the front of the shoe.

Enjoy your finished high heel!

*These instructions will make one finished high heel. Fold another one to make a pair!

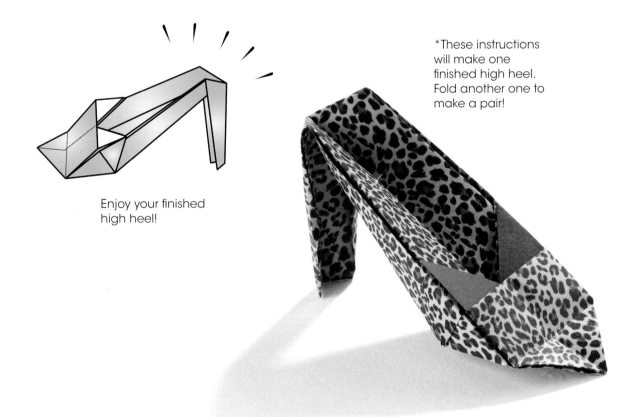

SWIMSUIT

Swimsuits have had a long evolution, from early bathing suits with long sleeves and skirts designed to shield skin from the sun to the itty-bitty bikinis seen today. But a classic one-piece swimsuit, like this paper version, is always in style. A tapered waist makes for a flattering fit, and the fun palm print is trendy and modern. It could even be worn with shorts or a skirt!

STYLE TIPS

- Your swimsuit will pair perfectly with a comfy pair of flip-flops and a cool pair of sunglasses.

- Don't forget a tote bag to throw your essentials in when heading to the beach or pool!

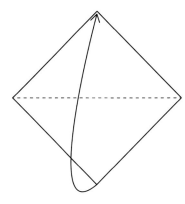

Fold the paper in half diagonally.
(Note: The side facing down will
become the pattern of the swimsuit.)

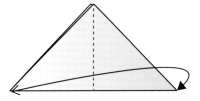

2

Fold in half again and then unfold.

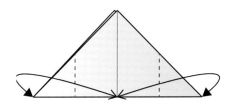

Fold the side corners into the
center crease and then unfold.

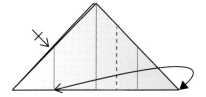

4

Fold one corner into the crease
made in the previous step and then
unfold. Repeat on the opposite side.

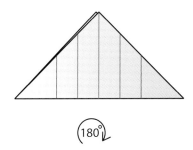

Rotate the paper 180°.

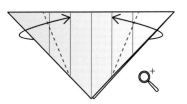

6

Fold the corners up to line up with
the crease made in step #4. (Note:
The next step is a magnified view.)

7

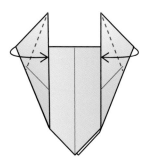

Narrow the corners by folding an angle bisector, bringing the outside corner in to meet the inside edge.

8

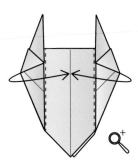

Fold the sides into the existing pre-crease. (Note: The next step is a magnified view.)

9

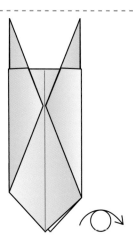

Turn the paper over.

10

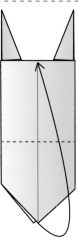

Fold the bottom corner up to the top edge.

11

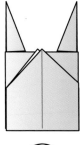

Turn the paper over.

12

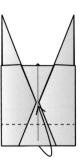

Fold the bottom edge up to where the corners meet in the center, flipping the back section to the front while doing so. This will create a pleat fold. (See the next step for reference.)

13

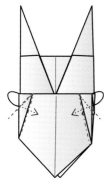

Inside reverse to tuck the bottom triangles in on the sides to shape the bottom of the swimsuit.

14

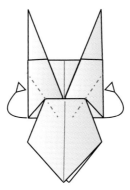

Mountain fold the corners to the back to shape the top section of the swimsuit.

15

Optional: Mountain fold the top of the swimsuit to make a V-neck.

16

Optional: Bring the two top points together and gently fasten them with a mountain and valley fold to create a halter top. (Note: This will not be a strong lock but rather a suggestion to help shape the top of the swimsuit.)

Enjoy your finished swimsuit!

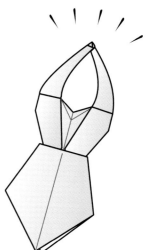

JACKET

Jackets don't have be formal! This origami version can be customized with different patterns or minor folding adjustments. Use a denim pattern to create a jean jacket, or choose a solid brown or black pattern for a leather jacket. You can also narrow the sleeves or leave out the cuffs depending on your personal preference. Draw in your own stitching details and pockets, or add patches and stickers to make it a one-of-a-kind closet must-have.

STYLE TIPS

- A leather jacket looks great with jeans, while a denim jacket can be the perfect piece to pair with skinny pants.

- Layer your jacket over different tops to create different looks—a T-shirt, blouse, or sweater will each produce a unique outfit.

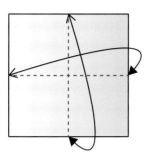

Fold your paper in half in both directions and then unfold. (Note: The side facing up will become the exterior of your jacket; the side facing down will become the interior lining and cuffs.)

2

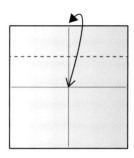

Fold the top edge down to the center crease and then unfold.

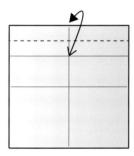

Fold the top edge down to the new crease created in the previous step and then unfold.

4

Fold the top edge down to the new crease created in the previous step.

Fold the top edge down again on the existing pre-crease. This will become the jacket cuffs.

6

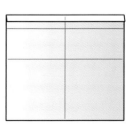

Turn the paper over.

7

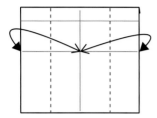

Fold the sides into the center and then unfold.

8

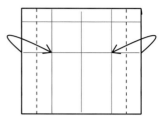

Fold both sides into the new creases created in the previous step.

9

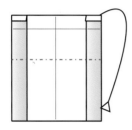

Mountain fold the top section to the back on the existing pre-crease.

10

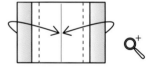

Fold the sides into the center crease. (Note: The next step is a magnified view.)

11

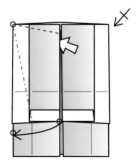

Working from the center, open up the pocket on the front layer and squash to form the sleeves. The creases will start at the top corner (as shown by the reference circle). Slide the front layers to the outside so the sleeve corner matches up with the side of the jacket. Repeat on the opposite side.

12

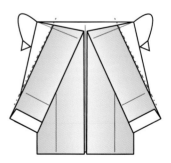

Mountain fold the contrasting triangles to the back to shape the sleeves.

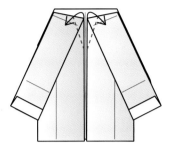

Fold down the lapels. (Note: You can make the lapels shorter or longer. Play around with some different styles and options.)

Mountain fold the top section to the back to shape the collar.

Mountain fold and tuck the bottom corners under to add detail to the bottom of the jacket. (Note: You can also alter the length of the jacket by leaving the bottom long or mountain folding it to the back.)

Enjoy your finished jacket!

ROMPER

The **romper** started off as a child's onesie, but these days it's a versatile garment that can be dressy or casual, depending on how you wear it and what accessories you pair it with. This paper version uses both sides of the paper to create a distinct top and bottom. Try folding it with different types of patterns and combinations for a variety of looks!

STYLE TIPS

⊕ Toss a sweater or jacket over your romper to take it from summer to fall.

⊕ Pair your romper with comfy flats for a daytime look or heels for an evening outfit.

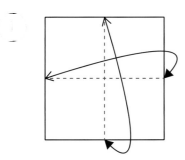

Fold the paper in half in both directions and then unfold. (Note: The side facing up will become the top half of your romper; the side facing down will become the bottom half.)

Mountain fold the top edge to the back to meet the center crease.

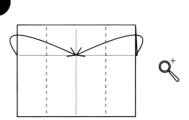

Fold the sides into the center crease. (Note: The next step is a magnified view.)

Fold the bottom edge up and then unfold.

Fold the bottom corners in and then unfold.

Inside reverse the corners.

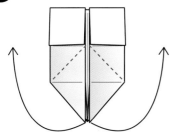

Pinch the bottom two corners in the front and pull out to the sides to make a boat shape. (See the next step for reference.)

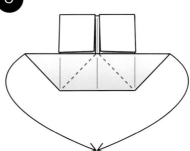

Fold the corners down to the bottom.

Fold the bottom corners up to meet the existing pre-crease and then unfold.

10

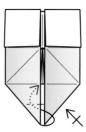

Inside reverse to tuck in the bottom left corner. Repeat on the opposite side.

11

Turn the paper over.

12

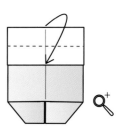

Fold the top edge down to the bottom of the top section. (Note: The next step is a magnified view.)

13

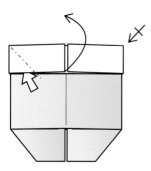

Pre-crease the corner, open the pocket, and squash fold. Repeat on the opposite side.

14

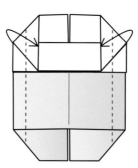

Fold in the side edges.

15

Fold thin triangles (through all layers) to separate the legs of the shorts.

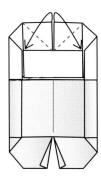

Fold down the center corners to create the neckline of the romper.

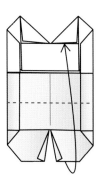

Fold the bottom edge up.

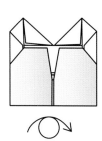

Turn the paper over.

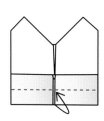

Fold up to create a pleat, bringing the back shorts section to the front while doing so.

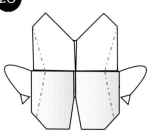

Mountain fold the sides in at an angle to taper and shape the waistline of the romper.

Optional: Fold the center sections out to create a decorative detail along the neckline.

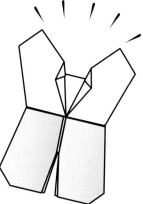

Enjoy your finished romper!

RAINCOAT

Raincoats make it easy to stand out, even in the midst of bad weather. Choose a raincoat with fun details to make sure your jacket is part of your outfit, not just covering it up. This paper version pops in a bright, bold red and has a leopard-print lining for extra pizazz. You can reverse the paper for an even bolder animal-print look, or choose a different paper and pattern altogether.

STYLE TIPS

- Toss your raincoat on over your sundress or shift dress to stay dry and stylish in gloomy weather.

- Don't forget to grab a tote bag to throw your umbrella in!

How To Fold

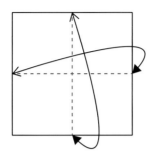

Fold the paper in half in both directions and then unfold. (Note: The side facing down will become the outside of the raincoat; the side facing up will become the lining.)

2

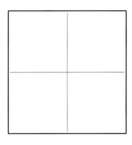

Turn the paper over.

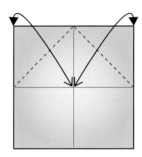

Fold the top corners down and into the center and then unfold.

4

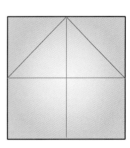

Turn the paper over.

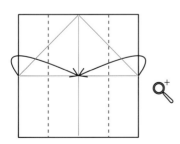

Fold the sides into the center crease. (Note: The next step is a magnified view.)

6

Fold the top edge down to the center crease and then unfold.

Fold the top corners down to the new crease made in the previous step and then unfold.

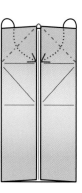

Inside reverse the corners using the pre-crease from the previous step.

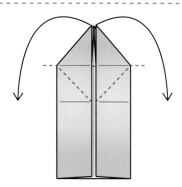

Pinch the top two corners in the front and pull out to the sides to make an upside-down boat shape. (See the next step for reference.)

Fold the top corners down using the indicated circle points as a reference and then unfold.

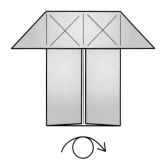

Turn the paper over.

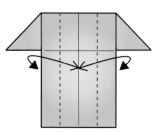

Fold the sides into the center crease and then unfold.

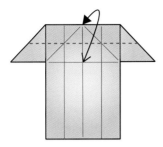

Fold the top edge down to the existing pre-crease and then unfold.

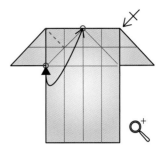

Fold a small diagonal crease on the upper, outside corner by bringing the circled points together and then unfold. Repeat on the opposite side. (Note: The next step is a magnified view.)

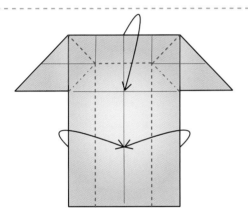

Collapse the model using the pre-creases. (Note: The next two steps are a detailed breakdown of this collapse.)

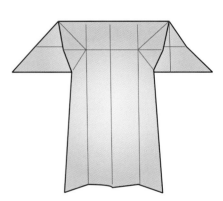

Fold the side edges in first, leaving the top section open. (See the next step for reference.)

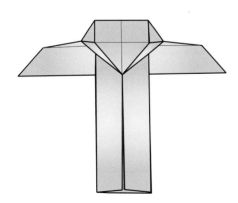

Fold the top edge down to make a long, narrow rectangle. (See the next step for reference.)

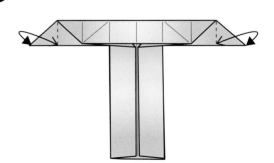

Fold the outside points in, folding the triangle in half, and then unfold.

19

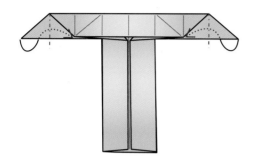

Inside reverse to tuck in the outside points using the pre-crease made in the previous step.

20

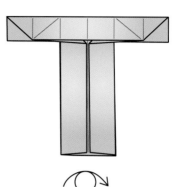

Turn the paper over.

21

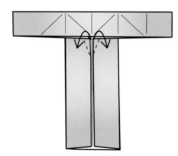

Lift up the top front layer and fold narrow triangles along the center opening to create the lapels of the coat. (Note: The top of the triangles will be underneath the front layer. See the next step for reference.)

22

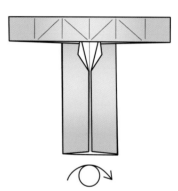

Turn the paper over.

23

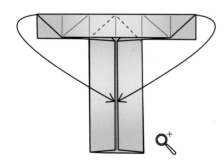

Fold down the sleeves. (Note: The next step is a magnified view.)

24

Fold the top triangle down to the front to create the hood of the raincoat.

25

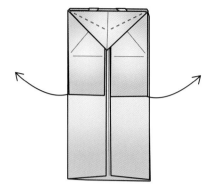

Keeping the top triangle folded, gently slide the sleeves out to the sides underneath. (See the next step for reference.)

 26

Turn the paper over.

27

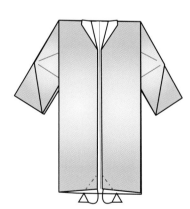

Optional: Mountain fold the bottom corners under for a more detailed look.

Enjoy your finished raincoat!

About The Author

Sok Song's passion for folding paper bloomed from a hobby he taught himself during childhood into an award-winning origami-design business called Creased, Inc. He later attended Parsons with the intention of incorporating his origami skills into garment construction and fashion design. Sok's work has been featured on numerous TV shows, including *America's Next Top Model* and *Extreme Home Makeover*. His work has also been included in magazines such as *Cosmopolitan*, *Elle*, *GQ*, *Harper's Bazaar*, *Icon*, *InStyle*, *Marie Claire*, *Pop*, *Self*, *Vanity Fair*, and *Vogue*. Other notable clients include Condé Nast Publications Ltd., Harrods, Macy's, Saks Fifth Avenue, The Museum of Art and Design, The American Museum of Natural History, and *The New Yorker*. Sok currently lives in New York City, although his folding work takes him all over the world.

Read More

Arcturus Publishing. *Fashion Origami*. London, England: Arcturus Publishing Limited, 2014.

Song, Sok. *Origami Accessories: A Foldable Fashion Guide*. Fashion Origami. North Mankato, Minn.: Capstone Press, 2016.

Savvy is published by Capstone Press
A Capstone Imprint
1710 Roe Crest Drive
North Mankato, Minnesota 56003
www.mycapstone.com

Designs, illustrations, and text © Sok Song 2016
Photographs © Capstone 2016

Library of Congress Cataloging-in-Publication Data is available on the Library of Congress website.

ISBN: 978-1-5157-1631-0 (library binding) — 978-1-5157-1652-5 (ebook PDF)

Summary: Ten original fashion origami models, including a variety of dresses, with written instructions and illustrated diagrams.

Editor: Alison Deering
Designer: Aruna Rangarajan

Image Credits: Photographs by Capstone Studio: Karon Dubke, Sarah Schuette, studio stylist; Marcy Morin, studio scheduler; Author photo by Alexanda Grablewski
Folding Papers Textures: Shutterstock: AlexTanya, Baksiabat, EvenEzer, Gorbash Varvara, Jut, maralova, Maria_Galybina, NataliaKo, OKing, Regina Jershova, Sunny Designs, surachet khamsuk, TabitaZn, Transia Design; Sok Song
Design Elements: Shutterstock: Baksiabat, BeatWalk, Ivan Negin, Iveta Angelova, Maria_Galybina, shorena, Svetlana Prikhnenko, tukkki

Printed and bound in the USA.   009684F16